The Rockwool Foundation Research Unit

Economic Drivers of Migration and Climate Change in LDCs

Helene Bie Lilleør
and Katleen Van den Broeck

University Press of Southern Denmark
Odense 2011

Economic Drivers of Migration and
Climate Change in LDCs

Study Paper No. 36

Published by:
© The Rockwool Foundation Research Unit and
University Press of Southern Denmark

Copying from this book is permitted only within
institutions that have agreements with CopyDan,
and only in accordance with the limitations laid
down in the agreement

Address:
The Rockwool Foundation Research Unit
Sølvgade 10
DK-1307 Copenhagen K

Telephone   +45 33 34 48 00

Fax   +45 33 34 48 99

E-mail   forskningsenheden@rff.dk

Home page   www.rff.dk

ISBN 978-87-90199-62-3
ISSN 0908-3979
October 2011
Print run: 300
Printed by: Specialtrykkeriet Viborg A/S

Price: 60.00 DKK, including 25% VAT

Contents

Abstract 5
1. Introduction 6
2. Migration in and from LDCs 8
2.1. Migration models 8
2.2. Taking migration models to the data 10
2.3. The typical LDC migrant 12
3. Climate Change and Migration 13
3.1. Climate change and migration drivers 19
3.1.1. Climate change and income levels 19
3.1.2. Climate change and income variability 25
3.2. Reduced-form estimates of climate change effects on migration .. 25
3.3. Climate change and strength of migration drivers 27
4. Discussion and Policy Implications 28
    References 31

Economic Drivers of Migration and Climate Change in LDCs

Helene Bie Lilleør,
Rockwool Foundation Research Unit[1]
and Katleen Van den Broeck, Esanas

Abstract

Environmental migration is a topic which has given rise to widespread debate and gloomy predictions about the state of the world in 2050, but where rigorous research and empirical evidence are unfortunately in short supply. In this paper, we review the existing research on and empirical evidence of how climate change and climate variability in Less Developed Countries (LDCs) affects two main drivers of migration identified by migration models in the economic literature, namely income level differentials between origin and destination areas and income variability in origin areas, and how they in turn affect migration. We find that there are serious gaps in both the economic and the environmental literature that render it impossible to make sound and robust predictions of how climate change and increased climate variability will affect the economic migration drivers, and of how these in turn may change existing migration patterns. There are some empirical indications that income differentials may increase due to lower income levels in the origin areas of LDCs, but virtually no evidence exists of the effects of climate change or increased climate variability on income variability. Furthermore, although a negative relationship between migration and rainfall has been established by many researchers, there is only very limited evidence as to what drives it. A clearer picture of the driving force behind the link between rainfall and migration would greatly benefit policy-making in this area.

Keywords: Migration; economic drivers; climate change; climate variability; LDCs

Forthcoming in *Global Enviromental Change* 2011

Acknowledgements
We are grateful for the advice and comments of the Foresight Lead Experts, Prof. Stefan Dercon, Tim Caudery, and anonymous referees. Any remaining errors are of course our own.

---

1 Corresponding author. Rockwool Foundation Research Unit, Sølvgade 10, 2tv, DK-1307 K Copenhagen. Web: www.rff.dk Email: hbl@rff.dk . All views are those of the authors and do not necessarily reflect the views of the Rockwool Foundation.

1. Introduction

Environmental migration is a topic which has given rise to widespread debate and gloomy predictions about the state of the world in 2050, but where rigorous research and empirical evidence are unfortunately in short supply. Predictions by Stern (2006) and others of up to 200 million 'environmental migrants' or 'climate refugees' have suggested the prospect of global mass migration induced by climate change, the popular media often adding fuel to the fire with images of people being temporarily dislocated due to extreme weather events (Laczko & Aghazarm, 2009). The debate has been flawed by the use of vague terminology, lack of conclusive empirical evidence, and absence of links to theoretical models of migration.

In this paper, we review the existing research on and empirical evidence of how climate change and climate variability in Less Developed Countries (LDCs) affects two main drivers of migration identified by the key migration models in the economic literature, namely income level differentials between origin and destination areas and income variability in origin areas, and how they in turn affect migration. Income levels are defined by the mean cross-sectional income of the area in question, whereas income variability is a measure of how much income fluctuates over time for a single household.

There are already several reviews of the general literature on migration. However, no review has yet been made of whether and how the main economic drivers of migration are affected by climate change. Although various papers relate different measures of rainfall and temperature to migration, surprisingly few analyse how changes in these measures weaken or strengthen the effect of migration drivers. We follow Deschênes & Greenstone (2007) in the definition of 'climate'. By 'climate' we refer to the weather in a location averaged over long periods of time, whereas 'weather' refers to temperature and precipitation at a specific time and place (Deschênes & Greenstone, 2007, p. 354). By 'climate change' we refer to a permanent change in the average long-term levels of temperature and precipitation, and by 'climate variability' we refer to a permanent change in the long term variance around the average levels, i.e. a distinction between first and second order moments. Climate change is expected to result in rising temperatures globally, whereas the effect on precipitation patterns will differ, depending on the location. Furthermore, it is also predicted that climate variability will increase with an increase in the frequency and intensity of extreme weather events (Hertel & Rosch, 2010). We concentrate on slow-onset climate change and increased climate variability as opposed to sudden climate change, although we will briefly touch upon the latter. Climate change, as opposed to environmental change, is thus global, and related to global warming. Environmental change is a broader concept which can be a result of, for example, oil spills or land degradation due to deforestation (Kniveton et al., 2008).

It is widely believed that LDCs in general, and Sub-Saharan Africa in particular, will be considerably more vulnerable to slow-onset climate change and increased climate variability than the developed world (e.g. Thornton et al., 2009; Conway & Schipper, 2011). Similarly, the debate on environmental migrants and climate refugees tends to emphasise predictions of mass migration from LDCs to developed countries. We will therefore review the existing research and empirical evidence of whether and how climate change and increased climate variability are found to influence migration in LDCs. In doing so, it is important to be aware of the types of migration analysed. Hunter (2005) distinguishes between forced and voluntary migration in response to climate or environmental changes. Sudden climate change typically involves forced migration or displacement, whereas voluntary migration may or may not be a result of slow-onset climate change. The specific focus of the review is thus on how slow-onset climate change or increased climate variability affect voluntary migration through their impact on the migration drivers.

To examine this field, we resort first to the key economic migration theories to identify the main economic drivers of migration: income differentials and income variability. We then review the empirical evidence relating to these drivers and the challenges the researcher faces when having to estimate their impact on migration. Subsequently, we turn to the research on how income differentials (or income levels in origin areas) and income variability have been affected in the past by climate change and increased climate variability, and how these factors have in turn affected migration.

Throughout the analysis we make one key assumption, namely that climate change, on its own, does not induce migration. That is, we assume that no individual will migrate simply because the local climate no longer accords with his/her climate preferences. An individual will only migrate as a consequence of climate change or increased climate variability if these affect his or her drivers of migration.

We find that there are serious gaps in both the economic and the environmental literature that render it impossible to make sound and robust predictions of how climate change and increased climate variability will affect the economic migration drivers, and of how they in turn may change existing migration patterns. There are some empirical indications that income differentials may increase due to lower income levels in the origin areas of LDCs, but virtually no evidence exists of the effect of climate change or increased climate variability on income variability. Furthermore, although a negative relationship between migration and rainfall has been established by many researchers, there is only very limited evidence as to what drives it. There are surprisingly large gaps in the literature and thus a clear need for further research in the area and for better national and international data with consistent measures of migration, climatic and income variables.

In section 2, we outline the migration models, their drivers, and how they are taken to the data. In section 3, we review the findings of how climate change and increased climate variability affect these drivers, affect migration, and affect migration through the drivers. In section 4, we conclude, discuss the difficulties of making future predictions based on the findings, and outline some policy recommendations.

2. Migration in and from LDCs

Before turning to the question of how climate change affects migration, it is important to have a clear understanding of what drives migration in LDCs. The migration literature is vast and several reviews already exist, e.g. Lalonde & Topel (1997), Lucas (1997), Taylor & Martin (2001), Lall et al. (2006), and Rapoport & Docquier (2006). We will therefore concentrate on outlining the main economic migration models, their drivers, and empirical evidence when the models are taken to the data.

2.1. Migration models

There are three main types of migration model identifiable in the literature, each with different economic drivers.

The first and earliest type identifies one key economic driver of migration, namely wage differentials between two areas. Rural-urban migration occurs when returns to labour are higher in urban than in rural areas (Lewis, 1954; Ranis & Fei, 1961). Later researchers described how wage differentials act as a driver of international migration (Massey et al., 1993; Lalonde & Topel, 1997; Bijak, 2006). The early migration models were based on the premise that migration occurred when labour markets had not cleared, typically in that there was excess supply of labour in rural areas at prevailing urban sector wages. The wage differential induces migration until wages net of migration costs in the two areas converge. As more people migrate to urban areas, the supply of urban labour increases and that of rural labour decreases, thereby reducing urban wages and increasing rural wages.

The second type of migration model originates from modifications to the original idea by Todaro (Todaro, 1969; Harris & Todaro, 1970). Todaro saw that rural-urban migration occurs despite high urban unemployment, and suggested that it is not actual wage differentials that drive the migration decision, but rather the differential in *expected* wages. Therefore, in addition to wage differentials net of migration costs, unemployment differentials and the discount rate of future earnings are considered to be drivers of migration. That is, a potential migrant weighs the wage differential against the unemployment probability and his or her subjective discount rate when deciding whether or not to migrate. Models based on

Todaro's work have been widely applied to international migration, for instance by Todaro & Maruszko (1987).

The New Economics of Labour Migration (NELM) models constitute the third type. They differ substantially from the other types in two key aspects: the introduction of rural risk as a factor in the migration decision, and the strong focus on the potential migrant-sending *household*, rather than the individual migrant, as the unit of analysis (Mincer, 1978; Stark & Levhari, 1982; Stark & Bloom, 1985; Stark & Lucas, 1988). Migration is viewed as a family strategy aimed at both maximising expected earnings and reducing the risk of consumption failure by diversifying income sources across sectors or agro-zones. Stark and his co-authors argue that in an environment where income is subject to large fluctuations over time, e.g. due to weather dependency, and where formal insurance or credit markets are nonexistent, having one or more family members migrate to a distant area with different income variability patterns (e.g. due to different weather conditions or availability of weather-independent income sources, typically in urban areas) enables the rural family to reduce the risk of consumption failure by diversifying income sources. This does, however, require an implicit contractual arrangement between the migrant and his family: '…an exchange of commitments to share income provides coinsurance' (Stark & Bloom, 1985, p. 175). The migrant's remittances insure the consumption of his rural family against local income variability;[2] and the family's resources insure the migrant against urban unemployment.

The three migration models thus identify two main drivers of migration: *(expected) income differential* between the origin and the destination locations, and *income variability*.[3]

---

2 Income variability is thus a measure of how much income levels fluctuate both over the year (between seasons) and from year to year, e.g. as a consequence of failed or bumper harvests. It is the variance of income over time for a single household, and not the variance across households at a single point in time.

3 It should be mentioned that relative deprivation has also been suggested as a driver of migration, since migration may be 'to improve the comparative income position with respect to that of other individuals or households in the relevant reference group (for example, the village)' (Stark & Taylor, 1991, p. 1163). As there is little empirical evidence of the existence of this driver, and none relating to climate change and increased climate variability, we will not consider it any further in this review.

2.2. Taking migration models to the data

A typical problem in empirical analyses of migration is that of establishing what the counterfactual outcome would have been – in this case, of knowing what the situation would have been if a given migrant had *not* migrated. Since migrants self-select into migration, they differ considerably from non-migrants in both observable and unobservable characteristics, making it very hard to find good comparisons among non-migrants. Likewise, it is impossible to say what the migration outcome would have been for those who chose not to migrate. Several researchers discuss this problem, e.g. Lalonde & Topel (1997) and Taylor & Martin (2001); and recently McKenzie & Yang (2010) have discussed the use of experimental approaches in overcoming the problems of the missing counterfactual and of self-selection in migration studies.

When applying the first two migration models to the data, the migration decision is generally estimated by regressing a migration variable (often an aggregate net migration flow when using macro data, or a discrete migration indicator when using micro data) on a set of explanatory variables representing drivers and barriers to migration, and on migrant (micro-level data) or country characteristics (macro-level data).

When using aggregate macro data on international migration, it is typically assumed that migrants and non-migrants receive the average wage and experience the average unemployment rates at the different locations, using simple cross-country averages. This is clearly unsatisfactory from an empirical viewpoint, since international migrants seldom enter the labour market of the host country on the same terms as the natives, but rather at lower wages and higher unemployment rates. Nor are the average wage and unemployment rate in the sending country appropriate measures of the migrant's opportunity cost, since it is often the more able and better-educated people who migrate. The impact of the wage (unemployment) differential on migration will therefore tend to be considerably over-(under-)estimated. Some of this bias in the estimates can be reduced by using cross-country panel data to take into account unobserved origin and destination country-specific effects; this is most carefully done in Mayda (2009). Like Hatton & Williamson (2003) and Clark et al. (2007), Mayda finds that larger income differentials between countries drive international migration, but that both immigration policies in the destination country and the demographic composition in the origin country also play important roles in explaining these flows.

Early papers using micro data indicate support for the Todaro hypothesis of expected income differentials driving *internal* migration. Among rural inhabitants of Botswana, Lucas (1985) finds that predicted urban earnings have a positive influence on their choice of migration to urban areas. Falaris (1987) shows similar findings for rural out-migration in Venezuela, allowing for multiple destinations and thereby earnings differentials. Likewise, the few papers on *international* migration using micro-level data find positive effects of income differentials on Mexico-US migration decisions, but also emphasise the importance of skills (Chiquiar & Hanson, 2005), destination networks (Munshi, 2003 and McKenzie & Rapoport, 2007) and cultural similarities in the Ecuador to US or to Spain migration decision (Bertoli et al., 2010).

Although some unobserved characteristics of migrants and their sending households can be controlled for when using micro panel data, it is hardly possible to completely circumvent the fact that migrants and non-migrants are inherently different groups of people without there being some source of exogenous variation in the migration decision. This is clearly pointed out by McKenzie et al. (2010) using data from Tonga-New Zealand migration, which is administered through a lottery for immigrant visas to New Zealand. With these data, the authors are able to establish the counterfactual of what happened to those who wanted to emigrate, but were not allowed to, using the lottery outcome as an instrumental variable for migration and thereby controlling for self-selection. The authors find that all conventional estimation methods clearly overestimate the income gains from migration, because they are unable to correct for the inherent selection bias.

Migration models of the third type, NELM models, are usually estimated using micro-level survey data, and the empirical analyses tend to take one of two forms. In the first form, the individual migration decision is explained by past income variability, indicating whether the household faces a high risk of consumption failure and therefore has an incentive to diversify income sources. Evidence of positive effects of income variability on migration is found in Rosenzweig & Stark (1989) and in Yang & Choi (2007); both of these use rainfall variations to instrument income variability, and they will therefore be reviewed in detail in section 3.3.

In the second form, the migration decision has already been taken when the analysis of risk-sharing evidence in the relationship between the migrant and the sending family is made. Evidence of how potential consumption variability triggers increased levels of remittances, and thereby invokes the insurance aspect of having a migrant family member, is found in the response to crop income shocks among households in the Kayes areas of Mali, where there is a strong tradition for emigration to France (Gubert, 2002); in the response to cumulative shocks among internal migrants in the Philippines (Quisumbing & McNiven, 2010); and in the response to domestic income shocks among overseas Philippinos (Yang & Choi, 2007).

Finally, it is worth noting that even with exogenous variation in income, it is impossible to extrapolate results from the type of empirical model described above to indicate what the impact would be if a different household member had been chosen for migration, or what the impact would be for non-sending households if they chose to let a household member migrate (Hoddinott, 1994; Rosenzweig, 2003; McKenzie & Sasin, 2007). The empirical findings should therefore be seen as upper bounds on what the true effects would be if both sending households and specific household members were chosen at random for migration.

Overall, there is considerable evidence that the two main drivers of migration in LDCs, income differentials and income variability, are both important for internal and international migration decisions. Although unbiased estimates of their true effects on migration are hard to come by, papers using exogenous variation from policy (e.g. migration lotteries), from natural (e.g. climate change) or researcher-led field (e.g. randomised information campaigns) experiments will often be able to come considerably closer (McKenzie & Yang, 2010). As we shall see below, the widespread use in the economic literature of rainfall deviations as such a source of exogenous variation in income has resulted in an interdisciplinary overlap with fortunate consequences for revealing some of the links between climate change and migration drivers.

2.3. The typical LDC migrant

The typical LDC migrant differs from non-migrants along many dimensions. Generally he or she tends to be a younger adult with relatively more resources in terms of financial, social and human capital.

Financial capital or assets are needed to overcome the costs of migration, which have been found to vary with the amount of social capital of the migrant or network size at the destination (Carrington et al., 1996). As the migrant network increases in size in the destination area, migration costs are lowered because new migrants get assistance in job- and house-search, just as larger migrant networks will lower the cost of adapting to a new culture and environment. Hence, the cost of migration may act as a barrier for pioneer migrants, but the constraint is relaxed once a migrant network at the destination exists. Examples of this are found in Mexico-US migration patterns (Munshi, 2003; McKenzie & Rapoport, 2007).

The typical migrant is often skilled, migrating to places where the returns to the human capital possessed are higher than at home.[4] This means that lack of skills acts as a barrier to migration, both internal and international.

Other barriers include physical and cultural distances, and strict immigration policies in the destination country (Mayda, 2009). Similarly, local exit barriers may exist. Social and cultural norms can dictate that migration is only accepted and facilitated for certain groups of people (De Haan et al., 2002; Beegle et al., 2011). Local land markets can constitute barriers to migration if they are thin, causing land owners to be less mobile because they are not able to reap the full benefit of their assets through sales (Lucas, 1997).

---

4 This may lead to a 'brain drain'. There is a large literature on this; see in particular Docquier et al. (2007) and Beine et al. (2008).

Finally, it should be stressed that the typical migrant is a (future) return migrant. Migration is often temporary, circulatory or otherwise non-permanent. This dynamic nature of migration is seldom taken into account when studying the drivers of migration. Migrants may be 'target savers', i.e. they return as soon as their savings have reached a certain threshold (Dustmann, 2003). Or migration may be part of an optimal life-cycle strategy, as suggested by Borjas & Bratsberg (1996), who argue that return migration out of the US not only occurs in response to changes in the discounted value of earnings, but can be planned as part of the migrant's optimal life-cycle. Similarly, using an exchange rate shock favourable to Philippine emigrant workers, Yang (2006) finds that most migrants can be classified as 'life-cycle' migrants rather than 'target savers'. This corresponds to the perception that many migrants return to take care of family members or of their inheritance, typically livestock or land (Lucas, 1997).

3. Climate Change and Migration

There are already several reviews of the general literature on migration. However, no review has yet been made of whether and how the main economic drivers of migration are affected by climate change or increased climate variability. Should we expect to find stronger or weaker effects of income differentials or income variability on migration? Do changes in means and variances of climate variables have similar or counteracting effects on migration drivers? There is a general lack of research in this area, and the questions above remain virtually unanswered. Although various papers relate different measures of rainfall and temperature to migration, surprisingly few analyse how changes in these measures weaken or strengthen the effect of migration drivers. We have found only one paper which does so explicitly: Marchiori et al. (2011). We return to this below. As we shall see, environmental studies are also virtually silent when it comes to analysing the effects of climate change and increased climate variability on income variability.

To create on overview of the existing (and lacking) literature on how climate change affects the two main drivers of migration themselves, and on how these drivers in turn are strengthened or weakened in their effects on migration, we divide the review into the following subsections. First, we consider the effects of climate change on the two main drivers of migration, as this will suggest the direction of possible secondary effects on migration. Secondly, we turn to the various studies which look at the 'reduced form' estimates of how climate change affects migration without being explicit about the driver. Finally, we review the papers where climate change affects migration either implicitly or explicitly through a migration driver. All papers reviewed are summarised in Table 1.

Table 1: Papers describing empirical evidence of climate effects on ...

	Paper	Country (Data sets)	Finding
A	**... income**		
1.	Ahmed et al. (2011)	Tanzania (Ministry of Agriculture/ Agro MAPS/ CRU TS 3.0)	Temperature has a significant negative effect on yields, while precipitation has a significant positive effect.
2.	Barrios et al. (2010)	Developing countries (IPCC/World Penn Tables)	Rainfall is a significant positive determinant of poor economic growth in African developing countries, but not in others.
3.	Dell et al. (2008)	World (Penn World Tables/WDI)	Higher temperatures reduce economic growth (levels and rates) in poor, but not in rich, countries through reductions in both agricultural and industrial output, aggregate investment and political stability.
4.	Dell et al. (2009)	Americas -12 countries (household surveys)	Negative relationship between income and temperature, both between and within countries (taking country fixed effect into account). Suggest that half of the strong negative short-term effects are offset in the long run through adaptation.
5.	Dercon (2004)	Rural Ethiopia (household survey)	Negative and persistent effects of rainfall shocks on consumption growth at household level.
6.	Deschênes & Greenstone (2007)	USA (Census of agriculture)	The effect of climate change on agriculture outcomes/profit in the US may prove to be much smaller than that found in other studies, when the adaptive responses of farmers are taken into account.
7.	Jayachandran (2006)	India (WB India Agriculture & Climate Dataset)	Rainfall shock is used in the first stage as an instrument for agricultural productivity. A positive rainfall shock increases crop yields by 7%.
8.	Kazianga & Udry (2006)	Rural Burkina Faso (ICRISAT)	Short-term negative rainfall deviations result in negative income shocks, which translate into negative consumption shocks with little evidence of smoothing or insurance.
9.	Marchiori et al. (2011)		See panel D below
10.	Rowhani et al. (2011)	Tanzania (national crop & climate data)	Both inter- and intra-seasonal changes in precipitation and temperature are associated with changes in crop yields. Increased precipitation variability reduces yields.
11.	Yang & Choi (2007)		See panel D below
B	**... income variability**		
12.	Rosenzweig & Stark (1989)		See panel E below

Migration type	Origin	Environmental measure	CC[a]
		Precipitation and temperature levels (not panel data)	Yes
		Rainfall anomalies[b]	Yes
		Variations in rainfall and temperature levels over 50 years	Yes
		Mean temperature and precipitation (artificial panel data)	Yes
		Rainfall shock defined as change in the log(rainfall) at t relative to t-1	No
		Variations in rainfall and temperature levels	Yes
		Rainfall shock (=level > 80th percentile of a district's normal rainfall)	No
		Rainfall deviations from long-run mean at village level	No
		Temperature and precipitation levels, and variability (not panel data)	Yes

	Paper	Country (Data sets)	Finding
C	... on migration, but not tested through an explicit driver (reduced form)		
13.	Barrios et al. (2006)	SSA and non-SSA (78 countries-1960-1990)	Climate change (proxied by rainfall) was a significant determinant of urbanisation in Sub-Saharan Africa but not in other developing countries.
14.	Beegle et al. (2011)	Tanzania (KHDS)	In an auxiliary regression, the authors find a positive effect of rainfall shock when a child on migrating as adult.
15.	Carvajal & Pereira (2009)	Nicaragua (LSMS)	Wealth, and whether the sector of origin is rural or urban, are correlated with the likelihood of migration.
16.	Findley (1994)	Mali (CERPOD)	There is a positive correlation between drought and internal migration and a negative correlation between drought years and international migration, but without controlling for individual or household characteristics.
17.	Gray (2009)	Ecuador (own data)	Less precipitation is associated with more internal and international rural out-migration, while an unusual harvest in period t-1 is associated with more local and internal migration.
18.	Halliday (2006)	El Salvador (BASIS)	The damage value of the shock (earthquake) was associated with a significant decrease in net migration to the US.
19.	Henry et al. (2003)	Burkina Faso (Population Census Survey)	Environmental variables are significant in explaining inter-provincial migration, but their contribution was slightly lower than that of the socio-demographic variables.
20.	Henry et al. (2004)	Burkina Faso (EMIUB)	People from drier regions are generally more likely to migrate. Short-term rainfall deficits increase long-term rural-rural migration, but decrease short-term international migration.
21.	Munshi (2003)	Mexico-US (MMP)	Uses rainfall history in origin community to instrument US destination network size. The auxiliary regression shows a negative effect of past rainfall on the number of migrants in the destination network, implying that lower-than-average rainfall induces more out-migration.
22.	Paul (2005)	Bangladesh (own data)	No evidence of out-migration in the aftermath of a tornado.
23.	Warner (2010)	Mozambique, Vietnam, Egypt (EACH-FOR)	Environmental factors (flooding in Mozambique and Vietnam, desertification and sea-level rise in Egypt) contribute to migration, especially via their effect on livelihoods.

Migration type	Origin	Environmental measure	CC[a]
Internal	Rural	Rainfall (level, normalised by LT mean)	Yes
Internal	Rural	Rainfall shock[c]	No
Internal and international	Rural Urban	Hurricane Mitch (1998)	Yes
International and Internal	Rural	Drought[d]	Yes
Local Internal International	Rural	Mean annual community precipitation	Yes
International (to US)	Rural	Earthquake	No
Internal, mainly R-R	Rural	Drought frequency, decade-to-decade rainfall variability	Yes
Internal, mainly R-R International	Rural	Rainfall from global monthly precipitation data (annual mean and short-term deviations)	Yes
International	Rural	Community rainfall levels with up to six-year lags.	No
Internal	Rural	Tornado (not panel data)	Yes
		Flooding Desertification, sea-level rise (not panel data)	Yes

	Paper	Country (Data sets)	Finding
D	**... on migration through the income differential driver**		
24.	Marchiori et al. (2011)	43 SSA countries	Climate variations increase the incentives to migrate internationally via changes in the wage ratio, but urbanisation mitigates the effect on international migration.
25.	Yang & Choi (2007)	Philippines (LFS, SOF, FIES, APIS)	Rainfall deviations are used to instrument income changes. Positive income shocks increase international migration, while negative shocks increase receipts of remittances.
E	**... on migration (or remittances) through the income variability driver**		
26.	Rosenzweig & Stark (1989)	India (ICRISAT)	Rainfall means and variances are used to instrument agricultural profit means and variances, which in turn are used to explain household consumption smoothing and migration.

Notes:
[a] Is climate change or environmental migration a focus of the paper?
[b] Rainfall anomalies = deviations from the country's long-term mean, divided by its long-run standard deviation.
[c] Rainfall shock: largest deviation of rainfall from 25-year average annual rainfall.
[d] Drought: % rain below LT 50 yr average in 1983-1985.
[e] Rainfall shock: Changes in local rainfall constructed as rainfall in year t in that season minus rainfall in the same season in year t-1.

Migration type	Origin	Environmental measure	CC[a]
International (+ R-U)	Rural	Precipitation and temperature (anomalies)	Yes
International	Both rural & urban	Rainfall shock (season specific)[e]	No
Internal (R-R)	Rural	Rainfall means and variances	No

3.1. Climate change and migration drivers

Although the term 'climate change' is often used quite broadly, there is an important distinction to be made between 'climate change' and 'climate variability'[5]. 'Climate change' is used in this paper to refer to a shift in the *average* temperature and rainfall levels, whereas 'climate variability' is an increase in the *variance* of these factors, with a corresponding increase in extreme weather events because the tails of the distribution get longer and wider (Easterling et al., 2000; Porter & Semenov, 2005; and Rowhani et al., 2011). It is worth noting that the variance of a climatic variable (rainfall or temperature) can increase without any change in the mean, and vice versa. Whether climatic changes result in shifts in both first and second order moments of, for example, temperature, or in only one of the moments, is likely to have different effects on the first (mean) and second order (variance) moments of the inter-temporal income distributions of households dependent on rain-fed agriculture. It is worth emphasising that the effects will not be direct effects of a changing climate on income, but a reduced-form effect driven by changes in crop yields, their threshold levels, available crop choices, and adaptive strategies. All in all, arriving at the net effects of climate change and increased climate variability on rural income distributions is a challenging task.

As we assume that income levels in the migrants' destination areas are considerably less affected by climate change than they are in the origin areas, we focus on the effect on income levels in the areas of origin, typically rural areas of LDCs. This allows us to look at the effect of climate change and increased climate variability on the first and second order moments of the income distributions at the origin, since changes in the first order moment (a shift in origin income levels) will proxy the income differential. As we shall see below, some advances have been made in trying to determine the complex relationship between rural income and climatic variables in both the agricultural/environmental and the economic literature. However, relatively little is yet known about the relationship of the second order moments, which we believe to be the most important for households living close to subsistence level, since even small increases in income variability can have dire consequences if the left-hand tail of the income distribution fattens.

3.1.1. Climate change and income levels

The analysis of the impacts of climate change on income levels is in itself represented by a large body of literature, including various reviews.

Morton (2007) reviews the impacts of climate change on smallholder and subsistence agriculture. He concludes that impacts will be very locally specific and hard to predict due to the number of complex, diverse and risk-prone farming systems

---

[5] Other terms are also used, such as 'climate volatility' and 'climate variation'.

in use around the world which feature a variety of both crop and livestock species in any one household. He emphasises the role of adaptive strategies: 'Small farm sizes, low technology, low capitalization, and diverse nonclimate stressors will tend to increase vulnerability, but the resilience factors – family labor, existing patterns of diversification away from agriculture, and possession of a store of indigenous knowledge – should not be underestimated' (Morton, 2007, p. 19684). He stresses the lack of the interdisciplinary research that is needed to understand how climate change will impact these farming systems, as farmers' adaptive strategies are many – adjusting the crop mix, production techniques, or land use, for example. Seo (2010) notes that in Latin America, switching to mixed farming systems rather than sticking to a specialised crop or livestock system can be a preferred strategy as a response to climate change. Similarly, out-migration of one or more household members for even larger diversification of income sources may also been seen as an adaptive or compensatory strategy of farming households. Households will always seek to reduce the negative effect of climate change and increased climate variability on household income by employing a range of adaptive strategies, some more successfully than others.

Hertel & Rosch (2010) offer a relevant and thorough review of how climate change affects agriculture and poverty in LDCs, drawing on both the agricultural/environmental and the economic literature. They examine the findings on how climate change affects poverty (or income) through the effects on agricultural crop production, profits and factor markets, taking the general equilibrium effects on prices into account. They distinguish between three different methodologies for estimation of the agricultural impacts of climate change: crop growth simulation models, statistical models, and hedonic models.

The crop growth simulation models are typically used for predicting impacts of future climatic scenarios based on data-intensive calibrations. They are field- and crop-specific, and therefore not built to take into account the perspective of small subsistence farmers in LDCs who employ a variety of different crop and livestock mixes for diversification purposes, typically as part of their adaptive strategies. Since the crop growth simulation models are highly calibrated, using inputs on soil quality, water availability, temperature, crop type, row spacing and so forth, they can show how a specific crop would fare under different climatic scenarios. These crop simulation studies seem to suggest that strong impact asymmetries of climate change on agricultural yields between the developed and developing countries may deepen the current consumption and production gap (which could increase the income differential) and that increased climate variability will increase yield risks (which could increase income variability) (Fischer et al., 2005). But several authors note that there are large degrees of uncertainty associated with these simulations for many LDCs and that there is considerable spatial and temporal heterogeneity in crop response to climate change (Challinor & Wheeler, 2008;

Thornton et al., 2009; Conway & Schipper, 2011). Furthermore, as farmers typically have more than one crop, as well as other income-generating activities, these models say very little about how the household income will be affected by climate change or increased climate variability.

The statistical models use broader regional or national data collection to examine realised agricultural and climatic outcomes. Out-of-sample predictions can be used to test their validity. Although these models cannot take the full range of compensatory response or adaptive strategies of the farmers into account, as not all of these may be in the observed data, they do account for the most commonly used adaptive strategies of the households in question. Their conclusions will, however, tend to overstate the damage associated with climate change, because less common alternative adaptive strategies are not considered (Deschênes & Greenstone, 2007).

The hedonic, or 'Ricardian', models assume that the value of agricultural production, and thus any change therein, will be directly reflected in local land values through perfect factor markets. Thus, economic impacts of climate change on the agricultural sector can be estimated by changes in land values, where the value of all adaptive strategies is taken into account. However, land may be put to a variety of uses not influenced by climate change, e.g. housing, and more importantly in poor LDCs land markets are typically far from perfect. Accordingly, these models have been substantially criticised (Hertel & Rosch, 2010, p. 8; Deschênes & Greenstone, 2007, p. 355), and we will not review them further as they provide little guidance in the LDC setting.

This leaves us with the statistical models. These have been employed both at micro and macro levels.

Macro-based statistical models

The macro-based statistical models tend to analyse the impacts on GDP growth and labour income of changes in temperature and precipitation. These macro models typical suffer from biased estimates, because unobservable country characteristics are hard to control for. The most convincing papers suggest that there are negative effects of temperature levels on GDP, but that these seem to be considerably mitigated in the long run.

Using the Penn World Tables (PWT) data for 60 LDCs from 1960-2000 coupled with IPCC data for rainfall, Barrios et al. (2010) find no effect of temperature on GDP growth. However, they do find relatively large positive effects of rainfall on GDP growth in Sub-Saharan African countries (but not in other developing countries), and suggest that this can be explained by Sub-Saharan Africa being more reliant on rainfall than other continents, due to its importance for both the agricultural and the hydropower-dependent energy sectors. However, this is contrary to the findings in Dell et al. (2008), who also estimate the effects of temperature and rainfall on GDP growth using PWT for a larger number (136) of countries. They find a negative effect of temperature on GDP growth rates and levels, but only in poor countries. They find no significant effects of rainfall. In contrast to Barrios et al. (2010), Dell et al. (2008) employ the method pioneered by Deschênes & Greenstone (2007) in using within-country year-to-year fluctuations in the climatic variable in order to partially overcome omitted variable bias due to other unobservable country-specific determinants of GDP. Barrios et al. (2010) use deviations from a long-term mean corrected by its standard deviation, and are therefore less likely to have overcome problems of omitted variable bias.

Aware of the possibility of remaining omitted variable bias due to country-specific effects which have not been accounted for, in a later paper Dell et al. (2009) employ a novel approach using detailed cross-sectional data from 12 countries in the American continents. Using municipality level information on labour income, precipitation and temperature, the authors are able to take both state- and country-level fixed effects into account when explaining the relationship between climate variables and income. They thereby establish that the often-found simple cross-country negative relationship between temperature and income is not driven purely by omitted country characteristics, though it is considerably reduced in strength. The magnitude of the negative effects of temperature on income is substantially smaller than those found on GDP growth (Dell et al., 2008). They therefore develop a simple theory to reconcile these apparent differences in the cross-sectional data and the panel data, and show that over half of the short-run effect of a 1°C increase in temperature is offset in the long run when taking the adaptive strategies of farmers into account (Dell et al., 2009).

Micro-based statistical models

Similarly, Deschênes & Greenstone (2007) find that overall there are only small effects of a hotter and drier climate on agricultural profits in the US. However, they do find a remarkable amount of heterogeneity across the country, with some states benefitting from climate change and others losing. It is therefore not surprising that both Morton (2007) and Hertel & Rosch (2010) conclude in their reviews that the relationship between climate change and the incomes of households that are dependent on subsistence farming is complex, most probably non-linear (e.g. temperatures above certain thresholds can result in sharp reductions in yields), and very locally specific. It is of course important what the starting point is for a change in the average level of either rainfall or temperature. Areas which are close to the upper threshold of, say, temperature for agricultural production are likely to suffer more than similar cooler areas. Likewise, already drought-prone areas will suffer more from further lack of rain than very wet areas, which may even benefit from such a change. It is therefore only logical that there are large degrees of heterogeneity in the impacts of a warmer and drier climate on income levels in different areas, even within the same country, and what may result in positive effects on income for some may have negative effects on income levels for others.

When it come to the net effect of climate variability (i.e. a change in the second order moment) on income distributions, matters become even more complex, and relationships less well established. Increased climate variability, one might expect, would translate directly into increased yield risk, with negative impacts on income levels and income variability. Again the starting point matters, and increased climate variability could result in a lengthening of the growing season, with beneficial effects on agricultural profits (Cabas et al., 2009). That said, both Rowhani et al. (2011) and Ahmed et al. (2011) point to negative impacts of increased climate variability in Tanzania on crop production and poverty vulnerability, respectively. However, there is a clear lack of research on this topic using statistical models, as most findings seem to be simulation-driven (Rowhani et al., 2011).

Additional findings stem from the economic literature, where 'rainfall shocks' are often a desirable source of exogenous variation used to instrument agricultural income variations.[6] The effects of rainfall measures on agricultural income measures are therefore not the main focus of these analyses, which typically seek a credible identification strategy for understanding the relationship between income and consumption. However, the analyses do still provide some useful findings for our purpose. Examples include negative effects of rainfall shocks on consumption growth in rural Ethiopia (Dercon, 2004), on crop yields in rural India (Jayachandran, 2006), on crop income in Rural Burkina Faso (Kazianga & Udry, 2006), and on household domestic income in the Philippines (Yang & Choi, 2007).

In conclusion, micro studies seem to find negative effects of rainfall shortages on income levels, whereas findings from macro studies are less conclusive on the effects of rainfall and temperature, though the latest study by Dell et al. (2009) does quite convincingly suggest modest negative effects of temperature increases on income. This calls for more micro-based statistical analyses using both temperature and rainfall deviations to explain changes in agricultural income levels.

---

6 Unfortunately, the definition of a rainfall shock varies from paper to paper, and is sometimes more closely associated with a change in the level rather than in the variability.

3.1.2. Climate change and income variability

We have found only *one* paper which implicitly analyses the effect of climate change and climate variability on income variability, in the sense that village-level rainfall means and variances are used to instrument profit means and variances, and that is Rosenzweig & Stark (1989). Since this paper also analyses the effect of income variability on migration, we will return to it in section 3.3.

Although intuitively it seems very plausible that increased climate variability will increase income variability, this is still an issue for empirical scrutiny. To the best of our knowledge there is, apart from the implicit analysis mentioned above, no empirical evidence related to this field. Thus, there is a clear lack of research into how climate variability affects both income levels and income variability in LDCs.

Even if the net effect of climate change on income levels is negative, it will be mitigated by the variety of adaptive strategies in place for most rural households in LDCs. From section 2, we can expect that a small negative effect on income levels should lead to a slight increase in rural out-migration; however, since we know only very little about how climate change and increased climate variability affect income variability, the net effect on migration could go in either direction. For instance, in a scenario with slightly reduced income levels, but where income variability is considerably reduced, one should expect less rural out-migration.

Before turning to the few studies which try to bring together the effect on drivers and on migration, we turn to the studies which estimate the composite 'reduced form' effect on migration.

3.2. Reduced-form estimates of climate change effects on migration

Excluding the theoretical possibility that some people may migrate because a changing climate results in local weather conditions which are not in line with their personal preferences, the effect of climate change on migration has, by definition, to be driven by its effect on migration drivers other than weather preferences. There can of course be other drivers of migration than the two main economic drivers listed above, e.g. migration for marriage, education, or access to services not readily available in the origin area, such as health services. However, in the vast majority of papers linking migration and climate change, the channel through which the effect of climate change is expected to impact on migration, i.e. which driver is likely to be strengthened as a result of climate change, is not subjected to empirical scrutiny. Rather, the 'reduced form' effect of climate change on migration is estimated, allowing the effect to operate through any type of unspecified migration driver.

Sudden and slow-onset climate changes may have very different effects on migration. Although slow onset climate change is the focus of this review, it is worth pointing out that sudden climate change is often related to disasters, and migration as a result of a disaster is likely to be forced rather than voluntary, as well as short-distance, temporary and internal (Naik, 2009). Paul (2005) finds no increased out-migration following a tornado in Bangladesh, and concludes that the availability and effective distribution of aid served to stem outflows. When international out-migration does occur, it has been found to depend on the availability of assets following both Hurricane Mitch in Nicaragua (Carvajal & Perreira, 2009) and an earthquake in El Salvador (Halliday, 2006).

Slow-onset climate change can be seen in changes to the means and variances of temperature, rainfall or sea-level. It is often a predicted sea-level rise that results in predictions of vast numbers of environmental migrants, simply because many large cities are coastal (Black et al., 2008). We have not, however, found any empirical studies based on existing data of the effect of sea-level rise on migration or its drivers; all the studies are based on simulations of future scenarios, e.g. for Egypt (Warner, 2010). Likewise, despite the importance of temperature for income levels described above, we have not found one single paper analysing the effect of temperature changes on migration; all the papers discussed below analyse only the effect of rainfall changes on migration.

All the papers analysing the reduced-form effect of rainfall deficits on migration using micro data seem to find evidence of increased migration. Rainfall shocks increase both the probability of people leaving the village and the distance moved in Northern Tanzania (Beegle et al., 2011). Less rainfall is also correlated with higher migration levels from Mexico to the US (Munshi, 2003). In Burkina Faso, people from drier regions are found to be more likely to migrate to other rural areas, both temporarily and permanently, than people from wetter regions. Short-term rainfall deficits increased their long-term migration to other rural areas, but decreased their short-term migration to distant destinations, emphasising the importance of distinguishing migration types by duration and destination (Henry et al., 2004). Similar destination-specific results were found in Mali in response to drought (Findley, 1994). In Ecuador, higher mean annual rainfall has been found to reduce both internal and international migration, but its effect on internal migration is larger. Additionally, consistent with the income variability driver, local and internal migration are found to significantly increase with fluctuations in harvest, but international migration is not affected (Gray, 2009).

At the macro-level, only a few studies relate rainfall patterns to migration. Again, results are supportive of increased internal migration in response to rainfall deficits. In Burkina Faso, a positive relationship has been found between out-migration and intra- and inter-annual rainfall variability (Henry et al., 2003). And in a study on urbanisation or rural-urban migration, Barrios et al. (2006) found that rainfall levels are negatively correlated with urbanisation in sub-Saharan Africa, but not elsewhere in the developing world.

There is thus ample evidence of a negative relationship between rainfall measures and migration, although it is hard to find any exact causal estimate of how rainfall influences migration, as all of the above studies suffer from selection and omitted variable bias. There seems to be a tendency in the literature to favour the income variability explanation over the income differential explanation, but on the basis of the findings in section 3.1 this appears to still be an area for further investigation.

3.3. Climate change and strength of migration drivers

As mentioned above, we have only found one paper which explicitly discusses how the effect of climate changes on migration runs through the income differential driver, namely Marchiori et al. (2011); and two papers which do so implicitly, namely Rosenzweig & Stark (1989), and Yang & Choi (2007).

Using macro-level data for Sub-Saharan Africa, Marchiori et al. (2011) find that temperature and rainfall anomalies *per se* (measured as deviations from long term trends) do not influence international migration. However, when they look at how the income differential driver is affected by climate anomalies, as well as the effect on urbanisation (which they argue acts as a push factor for international out-migration), they find negative effects of temperature anomalies and positive effects of rainfall anomalies for agriculture on a country's income differential compared to other Sub-Saharan countries, and they find a positive relationship between temperature and urbanisation. Controlling for these climate effects on the drivers in a second stage regression of international migration, they find an additional positive effect of temperature anomalies on international migration. It is likely that this could, in part, be explained by the income variability driver, which is not included in the analysis and which therefore, among other things, poses a problem of omitted variable bias in the estimated coefficients. The authors depart somewhat from standard economic migration models in their theoretical framework, which may explain the omission of several key variables compared, for example, to the empirical analysis by Mayda (2009). Furthermore, they are not able to convincingly address the standard problems of selection bias mentioned in section 2.2; the effect of income differentials on migration is therefore likely to be overestimated.

Marchiori et al. (2011) use IPCC climate predictions to predict the effect of climate change on future international migration from Sub-Saharan Africa and conclude that there will be large climate-induced migration out-flows. However, the fact that the estimates for simulating future migration scenarios are biased seriously calls into question the validity of these future predictions of migration. That said, the empirical analysis as it stands at present does seem to confirm the findings of Dell et al. (2008, 2009) that temperature deviations are more important for economic drivers of migration than rainfall deviations.

The two papers which implicitly study the effect of rainfall on migration both set out to analyse the migration decision and the effect of having a migrant family member on consumption smoothing when faced with an income shock, using micro panel data. Rainfall deviations are used to instrument changes in domestic income levels among Philippine households in Yang & Choi (2007), whereas village level means and variances of rainfall are used to instrument means and variances of agricultural profit among rural Indian households in Rosenzweig & Stark (1989). These are the only papers providing evidence related to all the different empirical aspects of the NELM model of migration as a family strategy – and fortunately, they do so in association with rainfall measures. These two papers therefore provide key insights into the effect of rainfall on income drivers. However, since their objective is not to explain effects of climate change on migration drivers, they do not discuss the degree to which the rainfall measures affect migration through the driver and whether there is any additional effect unaccounted for. The papers find evidence of (1) a positive effect of increased income on overseas migration in the Philippines among non-migrant households (suggesting that the households were facing a financial barrier to migration) and a positive effect of increased income variability (measured as profit variance) on internal migration and its distance in rural India; (2) a positive effect of fall in income on receipt of remittances among households with overseas migrants in the Philippines; and (3) a positive effect of having a migrant family member on reducing consumption variability in both rural India and in the Philippines, emphasising the role of the migrant as an insurer of stable consumption levels by providing remittances.

The findings in these three papers point to the importance of looking at the effect of climate change through migration drivers, and there seem to be indications of a strengthening of these drivers due to climate change; but three papers is obviously a very limited basis for forming strong conclusions.

4. Discussion and Policy Implications

In this paper, we have reviewed the existing research on and empirical evidence of how climate change and climate variability in Less Developed Countries (LDCs) affect two main drivers of migration identified by the key migration models in the economic literature, namely income level differentials between origin and destination areas and income variability in origin areas, and how they in turn affect migration. There are two main conclusions to be drawn from the literature reviewed above.

First, both of the migration drivers are likely to be affected by climate changes and increased climate variability in directions which would induce more migration, but existing empirical evidence is limited. There is some evidence of negative effects on income levels, but there is only very sparse evidence of the effects of climate change or increased climate variability on income variability, and more research is needed.

Second, there is also a surprising lack of research into how climate change and increased climate variability affect economic drivers of migration, and how their impact on migration is then either strengthened or weakened. Only *one* (very recent) working paper, Marchiori et al. (2011), has explicitly asked the question of how migration drivers are affected by climate change and how this in turn affects migration. Several studies have asked how climate variables affect migration, estimating composite reduced-form effects. Most studies find indications of rainfall deficits leading to increased migration, both internally and internationally, though effects on internal migration are considerably larger. However, since none of these studies identify the channel through which climate change affects migration, they are not very informative about how such effects can be mitigated. On the basis of the two studies which implicitly look at the effect of rainfall deviations on income levels and income variability, namely Rosenzweig & Stark (1989) and Yang & Choi (2007), it can be stated that there are some indications that the need for income source diversification is a strong migration driver and that remittances play a crucial role for most migration decisions.

On the basis of these conclusions, it is hard to predict how migration in LDCs is likely to be affected by climate change and increased climate variability in the future. However, there seems to be no evidence that points towards future mass migration from LDCs. The widely-cited projections of mass migration due to climate change of the Stern Report are not supported by any empirical evidence. These projections may even be harmful, because they misguide policy makers. Even if climate change results in an increase of income variability, it is likely that a large part of such an effect would be captured by already existing migration patterns aimed at diversifying income sources, and may simply just result in a larger flow of remittances, rather than increased (costly) migration. An increase in income differentials could increase migration, unless other adaptive strategies in response to a climate change are preferred. A strong effect of climate change or of increased climate variability on a migration driver does not therefore automatically translate into a strong effect on migration. And, finally, even if migration does increase, most migrants are internal and future return migrants.

Reflecting the research gaps that have been identified in this review, there has indeed been a general call for more interdisciplinary research made by many in the field (e.g. Morton 2007; Black et al., 2008; Laczko & Aghazarm, 2009; Hertel & Rosch, 2010). However, to do appropriate research and to be able to address the questions that remain unanswered as to how climate change and increased climate variability affect income levels and variability, more consistent data across and within countries would be helpful. In two excellent overviews of the challenges to the research and data related to the analysis of the migration-environment nexus, Bilsborrow (2009) and Kniveton et al. (2008) point to the need for putting existing data sets, typically household surveys, to better use, for instance by supplementing them with climate variables, as well as building new standardised migration modules to be included in future surveys along with a set of crucial climate measures. Laczko & Aghazarm (2009) take the lack of data so seriously that one of the major policy recommendations in their overview of migration, environment and climate change is the establishment of a Commission on Migration and Environment Data, which should develop standardised definitions and promote systematic sharing of data through an online clearinghouse.

Others point to the need for incorporating migration into the National Adaptation Programmes of Action, which are designed to help LDCs identify and rank their priorities for adaptation to climate change (Black et al., 2008; Leighton, 2009), and for developing national migration policies intended to facilitate and regulate internal and international migration, as in the Philippines (McKenzie & Yang, 2010).

Finally, development policies focusing on reducing fluctuations in agricultural production and overcoming market imperfections in the rural sectors will be important for increasing resilience to climate change. Such policies could include the spreading of new agricultural technologies, the introduction of drought resistant crops, better water access and irrigation. This could be complemented with the introduction of microfinance schemes providing micro credit, micro savings, and not least, micro insurance. The micro insurance should be weather-based, e.g. a rainfall insurance where pay-out is triggered when rainfall deviation reaches a certain size (Gine et al., 2008; Hertel & Rosch, 2010).

So even though the economic drivers of migration – income differentials and income variability – are likely to be affected by climate change, only the effect on the former has been established empirically. Moreover, even though a negative link between rainfall and migration seems to exist, it is unclear what drives that link. More data and empirical research into the matter to reveal whether the climate impact on migration operates through the income differential or income variability driver, or both, would be a valuable input into policy-making in the environmental migration area.

References

Ahmed, Syud Amer, Noah S. Diffenbaugh, Thomas W. Hertel, David B. Lobell, Navin Ramankutty, Ana R. Rios and Pedram Rowhani (2011) Climate volatility and poverty vulnerability in Tanzania. Global Environmental Change 21, 46-55.

Barrios, Salvador, Luisito Bertinelli and Eric Strobl (2006) Climatic change and rural-urban migration: The case of Sub-Saharan Africa. Journal of Urban Economics 60(3), 357-371.

Barrios, Salvador, Luisito Bertinelli and Eric Strobl (2010) Trends in rainfall and economic growth in Africa: A neglected cause of the African growth tragedy. The Review of Economics and Statistics 92(2), 350-366.

Beegle, Kathleen, Joachim De Weerdt and Stefan Dercon (2011) Migration and economic mobility in Tanzania: Evidence from a tracking survey. The Review of Economics and Statistics 93(3), 1010-1033.

Beine, Michel, Fréderic Docquier and Hillel Rapoport (2008) Brain drain and human capital formation in developing countries: Winners and losers. The Economic Journal 118, 631-652.

Bertoli, Simone, Jesús FH. Moraga and Francesc Ortega (2010) Crossing the Border: Self-selection, Earnings and Individual Migration Decisions. IZA DP No. 4957, Institute for the Study of Labor, Bonn, Germany.

Bijak, Jakub (2006) Forecasting International Migration: Selected Theories, Models, and Methods. Central European Forum for Migration Research Working Paper 4/2006, Warsaw, Poland.

Bilsborrow, Richard E. (2009) Collecting data on the migration-environment nexus. Chapter 3 in Laczko F. and C. Aghazarm (eds), Migration, Environment and Climate Change: Assessing the Evidence. IOM, Geneva.

Black, Richard, Dominic Kniveton, Ronald Skeldon, Daniel Coppard, Akira Murata and Kerstin Schmidt-Verkerk (2008) Demographics and Climate Change: Future Trends and their Policy Implications for Migration. Working Paper T-27, Development Research Centre on Migration, Globalisation and Poverty, University of Sussex, Brighton, UK.

Borjas, George J. and Bernt Bratsberg (1996) Who leaves? The out-migration of the foreign born. The Review of Economics and Statistics 78(1), 165-176.

Cabas, J., A. Weersink and E. Olale (2009) Crop yield response to economic, site and climatic variables. Climate Change 101, 599-616.

Carrington, W.J., E. Detragiache and T. Viswanath (1996) Migration with endogenous moving costs. American Economic Review 86(4), 909-930.

Carvajal, Liliana and Isabel M. Pereira (2009) Climate shocks and human mobility: Evidence from Nicaragua. Human Development Report Office, UNDP.

Challinor, A.J. and T.R. Wheeler (2008) Crop yield reduction in the tropics under climate change: Processes and uncertainties. Agricultural and Forest Meteorology 148, 343-356.

Chiquiar, Daniel and Gordon H. Hanson (2005) International migration, self-selection, and the distribution of wages: Evidence from Mexico and the United States. Journal of Political Economy 113(2), 239-281.

Clark, Ximena, Timothy J. Hatton and Jeffrey G. Williamson (2007) Explaining US immigration 1971-1998. The Review of Economics and Statistics 89(2), 359-373.

Conway, Declan and Schipper, E. Lisa F. (2011) Adaptation to climate change in Africa: Challenges and opportunities identified from Ethiopia. Global Environmental Change 21, 227-237.

De Haan, Arjan, Karen Brock and Ngolo Coulibaly (2002) Migration, livelihoods and institutions: Contrasting patterns of migration in Mali. Journal of Development Studies 38(5): 37-58.

Dell, Melissa, Benjamin F. Jones and Benjamin A. Olken (2008) Climate Change and Economic Growth: Evidence from the Last Half Century. NBER Working Paper 14132, Cambridge MA.

Dell, Melissa, Benjamin F. Jones and Benjamin A. Olken (2009) Temperature and income: Reconciling new cross-sectional and panel estimates. American Economic Review Papers and Proceedings 99(2), 198-204.

Dercon, Stefan (2004) Growth and shocks: Evidence from rural Ethiopia. Journal of Development Economics 74(2), 309-329.

Deschênes, Olivier and Michael Greenstone (2007) The economic impacts of climate change: evidence from agricultural output and random variations in weather. The American Economic Review 97(1), 354-385.

Docquier, Fréderic, Olivier Lohest and Abdeslam Marfouk (2007) Brain drain in developing countries. The World Bank Economic Review 21(2), 193-218.

Dustmann, Christian (2003) Return migration, wage differentials, and the optimal migration duration. European Economic Review 47, 353-369.

Easterling, David R., Gerald A. Meehl, Camille Parmesan, Stanley A. Changnon, Thomas R. Karl, Linda O. Mearns (2000) Climate extremes: Observations, modeling, and impacts. Science 289(5487), 2068-2074.

Falaris, Evangelos M. (1987) A nested logit migration model with selectivity. International Economic Review 28(2), 429-443.

Findley, Sally E. (1994) Does drought increase migration? A study of migration from rural Mali during the 1983-1985 drought. International Migration Review 28(3), 539-553.

Fischer, Günther, Mahendra Shah, Francesco N. Tubiello, Harrij van Velhuizen (2005) Socio-economic and climate change impacts on agriculture: An integrated assessment, 1990- 2080. Philosophical Transactions: Biological Sciences 360(1463), 2067-2083.

Gine, X., R. Townsend, and J. Vickery (2008) Patterns of rainfall insurance participation in rural India. The World Bank Economic Review 22(3), 539.

Gray, Clark L. (2009) Environment, land, and rural out-migration in the Southern Ecuadorian Andes. World Development 37(2), 457-468.

Gubert, Flore (2002) Do migrants insure those who stay behind? Evidence from the Kayes Area (Western Mali). Oxford Development Studies 30(3), 267-287.

Halliday, Timothy (2006) Migration, risk and liquidity constraints in El Salvador. Economic Development and Cultural Change 54(4), 893-925.

Harris, John R. and Michael P. Todaro (1970) Migration, unemployment and development: A two-sector analysis. The American Economic Review 60(1), 126-142.

Hatton, Timothy J. and Jeffrey G. Williamson (2003) Demographic and economic pressure on emigration out of Africa. Scandinavian Journal of Economics 105(3), 465-486.

Henry, Sabine, Paul Boyle and Eric F. Lambin (2003) Modelling inter-provincial migration in Burkina Faso, West Africa: The role of socio-demographic and environmental factors. Applied Geography 23, 115-136.

Henry, Sabine, Bruno Schoumaker and Cris Beauchemin (2004) The impact of rainfall on first-out migration: A multi-level event-history analysis in Burkina Faso. Population and Environment 25(5), 423-460.

Hertel, Thomas W and Rosch, Stephanie D (2010) Climate change, agriculture, and poverty. Applied Economic Perspectives and Policy, 32(3), 355-385.

Hoddinott, John (1994) A model of migration and remittances applied to Western Kenya. Oxford Economic Papers 46(3), 459-476.

Hunter, Lori M. (2005) Migration and environmental hazards. Population and Environment 26(4), 273-302.

Jayachandran, Seema (2006) Wage responses to productivity shocks in developing countries. Journal of Political Economy 114(3), 538-575.

Kazianga, Harounan and Christopher Udry (2006) Consumption smoothing? Livestock, insurance and drought in rural Burkina Faso. Journal of Development Economics 79(2), 413-446.

Kniveton, Dominic, Kerstin Schmidt-Verkerk, Christopher Smith and Richard Black (2008) Climate Change and Migration: Improving Methodologies to Estimate Flows. Prepared for IOM International Organization for Migration, Sussex University, Brighton, UK.

Laczko, Frank and Aghazarm, Christine (2009) Migration, Environment and Climate Change: Assessing the Evidence. IOM, Geneva.

Lall, Somik V., Harris Selod and Zmarak Shalizi (2006) Rural-Urban Migration in Developing Countries: A Survey of Theoretical Predictions and Empirical Findings. World Bank Policy Research Paper 3915, available at SSRN: http://ssrn.com/abstract=920498.

Lalonde, Robert J. and Robert H. Topel (1997) Economic impact of international migration and the economic performance of migrants. In Rosenzweig, M.R. and O. Stark (eds), Handbook of Population and Family Economics, Elsevier Science B.V., 799-849.

Leighton, Michelle (2009) Migration and slow-onset disasters: desertification and drought. Chapter 6 in Laczko F. and C. Aghazarm (eds): Migration, Environment and Climate Change: Assessing the Evidence. IOM, Geneva.

Lewis, W. Arthur (1954) Economic development with unlimited supplies of labour. The Manchester School of Economic and Social Studies 22(2), 139-191.

Lucas, Robert E.B. (1985) Migration amongst the Batswana. The Economic Journal 95(378), 358-382.

Lucas, Robert E.B. (1997) Internal migration in developing countries. In Rosenzweig, M.R. and O. Stark (eds), Handbook of Population and Family Economics, Elsevier Science B.V.,721-798.

Marchiori, Luca, Jean-François Maystadt and Ingmar Schumacher (2011) The impact of climate variations on migration in sub-Saharan Africa. Paper presented at CSAE 25th Anniversary Conference 2011: Economic Development in Africa, Oxford, UK.

Massey, Douglas S., Joaquín Arango, Graeme Hugo, Ali Kouaouci, Adela Pellegrino and J. Edward Taylor (1993) Theories of international migration: A review and appraisal. Population and Development Review 3, 431-466.

Mayda, Anna-Maria (2009) International migration: A panel data analysis of the determinants of bilateral flows. Journal of Population Economics, published online.

McKenzie, David and Hillel Rapoport (2007) Network effects and the dynamics of migration and inequality: theory and evidence from Mexico. Journal of Development Economics 84(1), 1-24.

McKenzie, David and Marcin J. Sasin (2007) Migration, Remittances, Poverty and Human Capital: Conceptual and Empirical Challenges. World Bank Policy Research Working Paper 4272.

McKenzie, David and Dean Yang (2010) Experimental Approaches in Migration Studies. Policy Research Working Paper 5395, The World Bank.

McKenzie, David, John Gibson and Steven Stillman (2010) How important is selection? Experimental vs. non-experimental measures of the income gains from migration. Journal of the European Economic Association 8(4), 913-945.

Mincer, Jacob (1978) Family migration decisions. Journal of Political Economy 86(5), 749-773.Morton, John F. (2007) The impact of climate change on smallholder and subsistence agriculture. PNAS 104(50), 19680-19685.

Munshi, Kaivan (2003) Networks in the modern economy: Mexican migrants in the U.S. labor market. The Quarterly Journal of Economics 118(2), 549-599.

Naik, Asmita (2009) Migration and Natural Disasters. In IOM (2009) Migration, Environment and Climate Change: Assessing the Evidence. IOM, Geneva.

Paul, B. K. (2005) Evidence against disaster-induced migration: The 2004 tornado in north-central Bangladesh. Disasters 29, 370-385.

Porter, John R. and Semenov, Mikhail A. (2005) Crop responses to climatic variation. Philosophical Transactions: Biological Sciences 360(1463), Food Crops in a Changing Climate, 2021-2035.

Quisumbing, Agnes and Scott McNiven (2010) Moving forward, looking back: The impact of migration and remittances on assets, consumption, and credit constraints in the rural Philippines. Journal of Development Studies 46(1), 91-113.

Ranis, Gustav and John C.H. Fei (1961) A theory of economic development. The American Economic Review 51(4), 533-565.

Rapoport, Hillel and Frédéric Docquier (2006) The Economics of Migrant's Remittances. IZA Discussion Paper No. 1531, Institute for the Study of Labor, Bonn, Germany.

Rosenzweig, Mark R. (2003) Payoffs from panels in low-income countries: Economic development and economic mobility. The American Economic Review 93(2), 112-117.

Rosenzweig, Mark R. and Oded Stark (1989) Consumption smoothing, migration, and marriage: Evidence from rural India. Journal of Political Economy 97(41), 905-926.

Rowhani, P., Lobell, David B., Linderman, Marc and Navin Ramankutty (2011) Climate variability and crop production in Tanzania. Agricultural and Forest Meteorology 151, 449-460.

Seo, S. N. (2010) A microeconometric analysis of adapting portfolios to climate change: Adoption of agricultural systems in Latin America. Applied Economic Perspectives and Policy 32(3), 489-514.

Stark, Oded and David E. Bloom (1985) The new economics of labor migration. The American Economic Review 75(2), 173-178.

Stark, Oded and David Levhari (1982) On migration and risk in LDCs. Economic Development and Cultural Change 31(1), 191-196.

Stark, Oded and Robert E.B. Lucas (1988) Migration, remittances, and the family. Economic Development and Cultural Change 36(3), 465-481.

Stark, Oded and J. Edward Taylor (1991) Migration incentives, migration types: The role of relative deprivation. The Economic Journal 101, 1163-1178.

Stern, Nicholas (2006) Stern Review on the Economics of Climate Change. UK Treasury.

Taylor, J. Edward and Philip L. Martin (2001) Human capital: Migration and rural population change. In Gardner, Bruce L. and Gordan C. Rausser (eds), Handbook of Agricultural Economics, vol.1, part 1. Elsevier Science, New York, 457-511.

Thornton, Philip K., Peter G. Jones, Gopal Alagarswamy, Jeff Andresen (2009) Spatial variation of crop yield response to climate change in East Africa. Global Environmental Change 19, 54-65.

Todaro, Michael P. (1969) A model of labor migration and urban unemployment in Less Developed Countries. The American Economic Review 59(1), 138-148.

Todaro, Michael P. and L. Maruszko (1987) Illegal migration and US immigration reform: A conceptual framework. Population and Development Review 13, 101-14.

Warner, Koko (2010) Global environmental change and migration: Governance challenges. Global Environmental Change 20 (2010), 402-413.

Yang, Dean (2006) Why do migrants return to poor countries? Evidence from Philippine migrants' responses to exchange rate shocks. The Review of Economics and Statistics 88(4), 715-735.

Yang, Dean and HwaJung Choi (2007) Are remittances insurance? Evidence from rainfall shocks in the Philippines. The World Bank Economic Review 21(2), 219-248.